Career Essentials: The Cover Letter

by

Dale Mayer

Career Essentials: The Cover Letter

Copyright © 2011 Dale Mayer

ISBN-10: 0986968269
ISBN-13: 978-0986968266

DEDICATION

This book is dedicated to Christoph, Jason, Nick and Kara, with thanks. Hopefully, the information found between these covers will serve you well

.

TABLE OF CONTENTS

ACKNOWLEDGMENTS

The Essential Series books wouldn't have been possible without the support of my friends and family. Many hands helped with proofreading, editing, and beta reading to make this book happen. I had a vision and without all of these special people, I couldn't have made it come to pass.

Thank you all.

INTRODUCTION

The cover letter is the beginning of everything. Whether you are applying for a job, looking for career information, or inquiring about a position, the cover letter is the first thing the recruiter or employer will see — it is your sales pitch.

This letter needs to generate enthusiasm and catch the reader's interest enough to motivate him/her to action: calling you in for an interview.

Cover letters are not limited to the job hunting world. They are utilized to propose products, services, and new ventures. As part of the Career Essential Series, this book focuses on cover letters for those people hunting a new job.

However, the principles of writing a dynamite cover letter are the same, and once learned, can be applied to any field.

Regardless of what you are trying to sell, which in the job hunting arena is yourself, you have to approach the letter with a marketing perspective. Key features need to be identified, such as your skills, abilities, and accomplishments. Then, you can understand how to communicate them to the reader.

Too often, the cover letter is ignored by job seekers.

1

Don't.

It is just as important as your resume and the differences between the two are huge. They are two separate documents with different strategies.

Consider the resume as a master document that can be reused time and time again. You will need to update and focus it depending on the industry and type of position you are applying for and you could have several variations, but it is a single document that gives a broad overview of your career.

The cover letter is unique to every person you are contacting and every job you are applying for. That means every letter must be customized to the situation and the recipient.

Don't forgo the value of a cover letter. It takes a little effort, but the end result is a professional application that can make the difference in getting that all-important interview.

In this book, the information is broken down into two parts. Part one is all about the cover letter, the types, the basics, and the essential components. In part two, each type of cover letter is discussed then followed by examples so that you can see the layout and the tone of each letter. There are several form letters that demonstrate how to fill in the blanks to create your own letter.

You should never copy a letter directly as you run the risk of making your letter sound like the million others out there. You want to stand out and be distinct from the other applications. The letter needs to show your personality, not someone else's.

It takes a little while to understand how to create these letters, and once you do, you'll find the process becomes easier with every one you write.

We're in a tough economy and it's important to do everything you can to find the perfect job. That means creating a powerful resume to showcase your talents and to write a dynamic cover letter promoting you as the 'right' person for the job.

Employers are struggling with an overload of applications for every position posted. They are looking for ways to sort through the piles and often, resumes that arrive without a cover letter will be the first to go. Don't be one of those. Learn how to make yours rise to the top.

Make it easy for the employer to see YOU as the answer to his problem.

How?

Let me show you. Grab a pen and pad of paper and let's get started!

DALE MAYER

1. COVER LETTERS

Frstly, let's address the issue of exactly what a cover letter is by definition.

Simply put, a cover letter is a document that is sent along with your resume to provide extra information on relevant skills and experience as they apply to the job in question.

The actual writing of a cover letter can be the most difficult process in your job search. Most people assume that everything is easier after writing the resume, which does take lot of effort, but consider: once the resume is written, it's good for several job applications. If the jobs are different from each other then, the resume needs to be customized for each job but, that is often a minor adjustment.

One generic cover letter is not appropriate for all situations. A new cover letter must be written individually for each job application. This is because you are always creating a cover letter for a specific situation, whether that is a job ad, a general letter of inquiry, or reaching out to a contact regarding a position. The situation dictates the information you need to include in your cover letter.

You need to customize or focus the letter to the appropriate area. If you are a customer service representative from a technical field, but are looking for a customer service position in a different industry, then you need to focus on your customer service skills, with the actual industry that you worked in being less important. The reverse is also true.

Each person's situation is different and each job will require individual treatment.

This is the only way to serve up the most impact and generate the greatest response.

A cover letter is meant to be a complement to your resume. It should add relevant information, not repeat what you have already said in your resume. You need to communicate the same information -- differently. If you copy the same wording, the recruiter will not appreciate you wasting their time. A cover letter should address as many of the points in the job posting as possible. Read the ads carefully as the employers often request information that needs to be included with your application. If you don't include what they require, your application is often tossed. Salary history or salary requirements are good examples of employer requests.

PURPOSE OF THE COVER LETTER

Your cover letter is one of the most important pieces of your job application. It's often overlooked as unimportant and sometimes disregarded entirely. Don't miss this opportunity to introduce yourself properly to your next potential employer. You wouldn't go into an interview without a proper greeting and nor should you send a resume without a cover letter.

Your cover letter is the first time the hiring manager is going to see your name for a specific job position. It is the first sample of your writing ability, attention to detail, and communication style. Make sure your introduction is everything you wish it could be.

Your cover letter needs to:

- Introduce yourself – you can be formal or informal but treat this as the first meet and greet moment.

- Make that all-important good first impression – it warms up your reception for when you do get to meet the employer.

- Emphasize why you want to work for that particular company, showing that you have done your research.

- Demonstrate how your skills and experience make you a good fit – the right person for the job through matching your skills and experience to the job.

- Show your focus, enthusiasm, and energy if you don't have much experience.

- Show your personality and eagerness as every employer needs to know that you are personable and enthusiastic about this position.

- Show what you can bring to the company and how quickly you will get up to speed in the new position – sell yourself.

- Focus on the company – your resume focuses on you.

- Demonstrate an understanding of what the company needs – and how you can help.

- Demonstrate communication and critical thinking skills by presenting a well thought out letter.

- Give you a chance to explain what may not be listed in your resume – such as when you're embarking on a career change. The resume lists your education and experience but not necessarily in a way that tells the story you want told.

- Offer new and relevant information – this is a great opportunity to highlight the information that the employer may pass over in the resume.

- Show the employer that you are capable of doing a good job. The letter is a demonstration of your skills, no matter how small, and shows an understanding of the process.

- Highlight your communication skills, which are important in any job.

- Explain something ambiguous or confusing in your history. A place to explain a change in career or if you've been out of the workforce for years, you can show what you've done to re-train, and stay current and up-to-date in the target field.

To be effective, your cover letter needs to grab the reader, engage his or her attention, and have them excited to bring you in for an interview. A resume is often restrictive in what you can put down. The cover letter gives you that chance to customize your application. This makes the cover letter a marketing tool. And like all marketing, how you sell yourself will have an impact on the type of response you receive on the other end.

TYPES OF COVER LETTERS

The terminology of the names of the various cover letters has changed over time. Some professionals will say there are three types, others will say there are five types, and still others will argue for another number. It doesn't matter how many there are, providing you use the right one at the right time. It's not complicated. To make it even easier, this chapter goes into a discussion of the various types, using names that are self-explanatory.

There are several general types of cover letters that fall across the full spectrum of the job hunting process from the beginning to the end, including:

1. Cold call letter – when you are sending out emails and letters (or going in person) hoping to generate a lead for a job.

2. Application letter – when you are applying for a specific job.

3. Referral letter – when you have a name of the person who referred you to the position.

4. Networking letter – when you are requesting job advice and/or assistance.

5. Prospecting letter – when you are inquiring about a possible opening at a company.

6. Follow up letter – written after the job interview.

7. Acceptance letter – for when you are planning to accept a job offer.

8. Rejection letter – for when you are planning on refusing a job offer.

There is a chapter on each type of letter with sample letters for you to see.

GETTING STARTED

Some people are good at sitting down with a pen and paper and writing a good copy the first time, but most people are not. They need to write a draft, edit it, proof it, walk away from it, and come back and realize it needs at least a word or two changed.

If you are one of the first group, good for you, as it means writing a cover letter won't be a difficult task. However, if you fall into the majority, you need to grab a pad of paper and a pencil and be prepared to spend an hour or two creating the best cover letter you can.

WHEN YOU'RE BLOCKED

Everyone draws a blank sometimes when they look down at an empty page and wonder how to begin. Some people call it writer's block. You can't fix what you don't have written in the first place. Therefore, it's important to get a start, any start, so that you can edit and revise it later.

How do you to start? If you are having trouble getting any ideas of your skills or achievements or even an understanding of how to begin the letter, here are a few tricks to help you get started.

1. Go to your resume, presuming you have already written a phenomenal resume to send out with your cover letter. Re-reading that document will help you develop the right words to use, as will re-reading any job posting you have. Look at your skills and achievements, your highlights, and your objective to see what it is you are trying to say.

2. Understand what it is about your career that you want to make happen. If you don't understand your own needs and how you want your career to develop then it will be difficult to make someone else understand.

3. Try writing down random thoughts on your career, skills, and accomplishments. Don't make any attempt to write coherently or in perfect English at this stage. Let the words flow and let the ideas pop up. It may only take a few minutes to have this happen or it may take hours. Don't rush it. Don't try to force this process. Take it easy and it will happen faster. This free writing will help to focus your brain. When the phrases start flowing, write everything down until they stop. Then sit back and see what ideas you have generated. There is usually something in this that you can then use to get started on your cover letter.

Another way to kick-start the process is to ask yourself different questions.

1. What kind of person would you want to hire?

2. What qualities do you have that you'd like him to know about?

3. What is your greatest accomplishment?

4. What skills are you the most proud of having acquired?

5. What can you do for the company that another person can't?

6. How do your skills match the requirements of the company?

If you researched the company, consider the following questions:

1. What is it about the company you admire?

2. What do you like about the position?

3. Which of the listed requirements are your strongest?

4. Which of the listed requirements are your weakest?

After going over these types of answers, you'll have a good start at collecting the material you need to write a dynamite letter.

TIPS FOR ALL COVER LETTERS

There are certain basic elements to all business correspondence that everyone should follow. Let's go over the most important tips as they relate to the cover letters.

1. Do use standard business letter format and not a quickly jotted down note.

2. Follow proper grammar, whether you send by email or mail. Never use text message language.

3. Do state why you think the company is one you'd like to work for. Show in some way that you admire who they are. You should have done research on this company first, and from that, you will find a

statement that shows your understanding of who they are and what they do.

4. Write in an easy to read conversational style. You may have five degrees and know your field of expertise well, but this letter is going to a hiring manager and it needs to show your communication skills. That means to avoid using jargon, long uncommon words, or complex language. Avoid being arrogant or superior in your tone of voice.

5. Direct the letter to the right person, use his/her name properly, and be sure to double check the spelling of the person's name, position, and the company they work for.

6. Make the letter original to each person you are contacting. Do not send out a form letter to everyone.

7. Explain why you are writing this letter. Avoid doing this in the first line, instead use a subject line in the letter or if emailing, in the subject line of the email. Make it clear by stating a job number if available, the position, or any other pertinent information to avoid having the reader wonder who you are and why you've contacted him.

8. Use the same type of paper for the cover letter and envelope as you used for your resume.

9. Make the letter short, concise, and specific so that you hold the reader's attention.

10. Don't lie. Only put down in your letter what you can back up. Don't exaggerate your skills or abilities.

11. Open with a strong introduction that will make the readers take notice.

12. Focus your letter on the employer and his needs.

13. It's easy for an employer to ignore most letters, so answer his needs with your skills in such a way that he will want to know more.

14. Sell yourself by answering the question that the readers will ask themselves, "What's in it for my company?" You need to show them how hiring you will benefit them. Show them what you've done and how you skills will benefit the employer. Remember that employers are looking for people that give results. They want facts and figures that clearly state your accomplishments.

15. Do be polite in all your communications. Don't write anything that could be taken as racist or controversial in any way.

16. Finish the letter with an action closing that reinforces your enthusiasm, your belief that you are the right person, and that you would like to have an interview. This is where you will call them in a few days.

17. Proofread, proofread, and then print the cover letter off and do it again. Don't rely on spell check to catch all the errors. Even better, have someone else read over the letter to see what errors they can find. You need to send out as perfect a copy of the letter as possible. This is your first presentation, so make it a good one.

Always do a follow up. Wait a few days after emailing, and a week or more after mailing your cover letter and resume, then contact the employer as a follow up to your letter.

QUICK NOTE ON LETTER STYLES

In today's business world, most letters are done in block letter style. This means that everything lines up at the left side of the page. The date follows the return address, and then two blank lines followed by the employer's name and address. There is one line and the salutation is next. The body of the letter is separated by a single blank line. A single blank line separates the last line of the last paragraph from the closing, which is followed by several more lines and then the signature.

2. THE BASICS

Each person has a different skill level when it comes to writing a letter. For that reason, here is a short section on the basics to help everyone start from the same position.

GRAMMAR

A cover letter is your first introduction, and the first opportunity to show your communication skills to the potential employer. It's essential that you utilize good grammar. If you need to review basic grammar skills before starting your job search, then do so. You don't want to find out after the fact that your English skills are the reason you haven't been called in for interviews.

If your skills are close enough that you feel studying is a waste of time, consider having a friend proofread your cover letter to make sure he or she doesn't spot any glaring mistakes that you might have missed.

As a quick review, be sure to check:

- **Abbreviations** – double check the abbreviations that you put down or avoid using any altogether. Don't make up an abbreviation. Prior to using one for the first time, you have to spell out the word fully then put the abbreviation in brackets. This only applies to the first time you use the abbreviation. A portable document file (PDF) is an example. If your skills require listing abbreviations that are self-explanatory by others in the industry you don't need to explain, such as HTML instead of writing out HyperText Markup Language (HTML). A cover letter is all about understanding the audience.

- **Capitalization** – this is another area that often confuses people. Trade names and proper nouns like company names all require capitalization. An official department, agency, or organization should be capitalized. For example U.S. Department of Energy is correct. If you are using a word in a general sense, such as…in my last company…the word company is not capitalized.

- **Fragment** – do use complete sentences at all times. Fragments, which are common in fiction, are not proper in any kind of business documents. They are incomplete thoughts and should be avoided. The easiest way to understand if a sentence is correct is to say it out loud. A fragment sounds like an incomplete thought.

- **Long** – Just as incomplete sentences aren't allowed, overly long or run-on sentences are also not recommended. Keep your sentences short and simple and you'll avoid both problems.

- **Numbers** – are another problem for many people and it becomes an even bigger problem when there are two numbers together, such as:

Oversaw six 4-member teams or ran two 24 line switchboards

The easiest way to avoid the confusion is by rewriting the numbers in another way.

Oversaw two switchboards with 24 lines each

Remember to always start a sentence with a word; if it must be a number then spell it out.

PUNCTUATION

Punctuation is another problem for many people. These types of mistakes will make your letter appear amateurish instead of showing you as a consummate professional.

Again, if your knowledge in this area is weak, then either brush up by doing some practice exercises or get assistance. This Owl Purdue Online Writing Lab (http://owl.english.purdue.edu/) is particularly helpful. Here are a few basics:

- **Periods** – a period is at the end of every sentence.

- **Commas** – comma misuse is another problem. Read the sentence aloud and wherever you pause is a best guess for a comma. There are over two hundred rules defining commas, but this generalization will help you get through a cover letter.

- **Semicolons** – a good way to look at semi-colons is as a weak period or as a severe comma. If you can't use them appropriately, then avoid them altogether.

Where you were considering a semi-colon, use a period instead.

- **Hyphens** – sometimes you need to use hyphens to keep connected words together for clarity. Think about the phrase 'a first-rate student.' Without the hyphen the three words mean something totally different. The same for words like thirty-eight, without the hyphen the meaning becomes unclear. Use them sparingly but as needed.

SKILLS

The skills in your cover letter are the essence of what you have to offer. It's these the employer is looking for. In order to attract his attention, you need to pay attention to how you communicate your skills.

Skills can be broken down into several different categories. You need to understand them so that you can demonstrate your knowledge and expertise in any of them.

BASIC SKILLS

At this level, we're looking at the basics of reading, writing, and arithmetic. Add to that basic computer skills, given the age of technology, and you can easily see that these are the skills of getting along in life regardless of the type of job you do.

Most people forget to consider these skills. However, given the high population of mixed languages, it's important for the employer to know that you can do these things.

Reading – all jobs, in theory, require a certain level of reading skills. Consider that you might need to read manuals or training guides or even fill out a time sheet to get paid on time.

Writing – you need to be able to write reports in such a way as to communicate your thoughts or for test results. Most jobs require some level of writing skills in one or more languages.

Math skills – it's hard to imagine any type of position that doesn't require some basic math skills. Think about problem solving, keeping a ledger or using a calculator on the computer.

Speaking – even if you aren't looking for a position in public speaking, realize that all jobs require you to communicate with your supervisors, peers, and potential customers. Good speaking skills are essential to being understood.

Listening – it's hard to imagine this as a skill unless you think about the people around you who don't listen to instructions or who sleep through all the staff meetings.

Social – these are how you get along with others. Do you respect others? Can you stand up for yourself? Do you take an interest in others or do you follow other people?

Leadership – this shows how well you can motivate, encourage, and convince other people to act and to trust you.

Teamwork – how do you work with other people? Can you contribute ideas and do your share the work or do you back off and let others do it all?

Negotiation – having the ability to understand the give and take in relationships, present the facts and arguments of your position while understanding each role in a discussion so as to minimize conflict and create compromise is highly regarding by employers.

Beyond these types of skills, employers are looking for people with the ability to:

- Make decisions
- Think creatively
- Solve problems
- Be trainable
- Be responsible
- Have reasonable self-esteem

DESIRABLE SKILLS

A cover letter is your opportunity to highlight relevant skills the employer is looking for. The types of skills that are important to all employers include:

Job related – these are the skills that assure an employer that you can do the job. They are sometimes called technical or professional skills. These are specific to your industry, such as having C++ for programmers, or CAD modelling for draftsmen, and financial planning for accountants.

Marketable – these are the ones that an employer is willing to pay you for. They are the ones listed in the job ad that the company needs to function. Think of unmarketable skills as the opposite. You might be good at something but that doesn't mean someone is willing to pay you do it. An example of an unmarketable skill would be to fly a kite for 10 hours without it coming down.

Adaptive – these are harder to define as they deal with personality traits and characteristics that help determine the way you work. Included in this group are honesty, reliability, and productivity.

Transferable – these are skills that can move from one job to another such as communication, teamwork, negotiating, and managing.

ACTION WORDS

Always use action words to highlight your skills. There are hundreds of words to choose from. Included in this list are power words like analyzed, achieved, built, coordinated, generated, managed, negotiated, obtained, and even illustrated.

Once you understand that these are verbs and think about the jobs you have worked in the past, it becomes much easier to find the right words to put down.

Full lists of action words can be found in several places. Searching with Google will bring up many options, but a couple websites to check are:

- http://info.piercecollege.edu/offices/jobcenter/library/action.pdf
- http://www.quintcareers.com/action_skills.html
- http://www.writeexpress.com/action—verbs.html

ACTION WORD STATEMENTS

This is a list from my Career Essentials: The Resume book. Don't use these exactly as they are written here. Instead, use them as a blueprint to create your own.

- Analyzed overall efficiency and monitored outcomes based on Quality Control goals on full line of company products.

- Applied new business model to existing company to increase sales by 15% and decrease expenses by an additional 12%.

- Built prototypes for hydraulic jack systems for the automotive industry.

- Coordinated activities for 200 volunteers, including speakers, accommodations, and meals.

- Designed and implemented a new document management system to secure the intellectual property of the company.

- Guided 120 employees through implementation of new business process.

- Headed four committees for the new hospital to establish new policies, strategies, and methodology as day-to-day operations started.

- Motivated employees to complete the time management guidelines put in place by new board members.

- **Simplified** accounting processes and payroll system for company and its two sister companies.

- **Wrote** documentation on company policy and procedures.

3. THE ESSENTIAL PIECES

If you break a cover letter down to the essential parts, you'll be able to tackle each paragraph separately. The instructions here apply to both standard letters that are mailed and letters that are emailed. There are a few differences between these two and they are laid out in Chapter 4: Emailing versus mailing.

THE ADDRESS

The rules on a standard business letter format say that you should put your name, house address, city, state, ZIP code, telephone, and email address. This is nothing new to most of you, so let's go through the material as a refresher for those people who have no experience in writing business letters. Always use standard format such as:

Your name
Street address
City, State, ZIP

Phone number
Email address

Below this, skip a line and write down the date that you are writing the letter.

Skip a line and then write down the name and the address of the person you are writing to. List the person's full name, on the next line goes the position title, followed by company name, the company address, City, State, and ZIP so it looks like this:

Your name
Street address,
City, State, ZIP
Phone number
Email address

Date

Name
Title
Company name
Company address
City, State, Zip

There are variations on this format, but this one will do every situation.

THE SALUTATION

In a standard business letter, you always use a formal salutation such as Dear Mr. or Ms. followed by the person's last name.

Be sure to have the correct spelling of the person's name. For those of you still confused over the use of Ms., Miss, or Mrs., understand that only Ms. is appropriate for written business use UNLESS you have correspondence from the person that specifically shows you how they like to be addressed. Also do address the person using only his/her last name so *Mr. Smith* and not *John Smith* or *Mr. John Smith*.

If the person in question uses the title of Dr. then you should use it. Not everyone does, so don't presume. Instead, do some research and try to find out. The company website is always a good place to start looking for this type of information.

A problem may arise when the name of the person you are addressing doesn't give a hint of the gender of the person in question. In this case, research is required. Start with the company website, and then move to searching via the Internet. This person could have won an award or written various articles where you may find out this information. If you can't find out, then pick up the phone and call the company. Tell them you are writing a letter and need the correct way to address this person. Be polite, ask for the correct spelling of this person's name, and be sure to write the answer down. Other professionals suggest using the full name should the person's gender be unknown, such as ***Dear Janhal Omire.***

What if there is no name? The first thing is to call and see if you can find the correct person to address the letter to. If you can't find out, then you need to fall back onto the old standby of Dear Sir or Madam. This is definitely only a last resort.

Another last resort alternative is to address the letter to 'Dear Human Resources Manager, or Dear Hiring Manager.' In both these cases, you should be able to call the company and find the name of the person to properly address the letter. If however, the job is closing soon and it's past business hours, this may be your only alternative.

The problem with these last resort solutions is that you will end up looking like many other people who haven't taken the time to do their homework. This type of address can also make it look like you have just finished a massive mail out of the same form letter to everyone on a list.

The idea is to set yourself above the competition, not put yourself right in the middle of it.

The following are common options:

Dear Sir/Madam – this is a generic option and inoffensive. It could be considered old-fashioned.

To Whom It May Concern – this is a standard option but is impersonal and could also be considered old-fashioned.

Dear Human Resources – other variations include Hiring Committee, Human Resources Representative. These are fine if you are answering an ad that doesn't list a name, just an address.

Dear Sir – not recommended as it's often wrong.

No salutation – this is fine for a job ad where there is no name given as to whom to address the letter.

Good Morning – this is conversational in tone and works for a basic ad but isn't always received nicely. Sounds like spam.

THE PUNCTUATION

Traditionally, proper business punctuation for a formal business letter such as a cover letter would require a colon after the salutation, such as:

Dear Mr. Smith:

Dear Board of Directors:

However, in less formal style business letters, a comma after the salutation is appropriate, such as

Dear John,

John Smith,

There is a trend to de-formalize the process somewhat and you will see more and more cover letters with only a comma after the salutation. Both are acceptable depending on what you find comfortable.

REFERENCE LINE

Instead of wasting your opening sentence by stating where you found out about the job or what you are applying for, feel free to make use of the reference line, which can go either below the date or below the hiring manager's address.

Always put the line on the left side of the letter and start with Re: so it looks like this –

Re: Job number J4322

It is normal to include a reference line if you are asked to quote specific information such as a job reference number. You can also use it to identify the type of job you are applying for or the location of the job post.

Re: Office Manager Position posted on Craigslist

OPENING LINE

With the name of the position title, and/or job number noted on the reference line, you can then make good use of this opening sentence to grab the employer's attention. Too often a cover letter is only glanced at and tossed in the garbage. You have only a couple of seconds to catch their attention.

Having said that, don't attract attention the wrong way by not using proper English and being unprofessional. This introduction is a statement of your personality. If your personality is a little out of the box, and that's what you want to advertise, and you will be the same person in the interview, then do so. If you aren't in a sales or artistic field then you may want to stay with a more subdued opening.

Use words in your opening sentence that mean something to the employer. This is where you:

1. Mention if you have a referral from an employee of the company or from a friend that they would know. If you have either of these, it can open many doors. Put this person's full name in the opening statement. Consider adding the person's department or position if the company is very large. Many people are uncomfortable name-dropping; however, it almost guarantees that your cover letter will get read.

2. If you are associated with a recognizable and related group, put that in your opening statement.

3. If you don't have either of the above, then start by explaining why you are contacting this person. State what you want and then follow up with what you have to offer. Only put in qualifications or skills that apply to the job requirements.

4. Make a statement that will keep the reader reading.

There are many standard openings and it is best if you don't use the same tired openings as everyone. Do NOT copy any of these.

Some are common, you'll recognize them yourself. Read the following suggestions and adapt them to your own use:

1. Jason Brooke from the Ingersoll Warehouse Division suggested I contact you regarding an office manager's position open in your Portland office.

2. As an author and journalist...

3. I'm excited to hear about the new job opening in the accounting department of your firm...

4. Please accept my application for the position of...

5. As a recent graduate of UBC Engineering program, I am applying for a junior engineer position in your company...

6. Are you looking for an employee that has _____ with the ability to _____? If so...

7. From my attached resume, you will see that I have ____ years of experience in _____ and am skilled in _____.

8. I attended the job fair at UBC yesterday and was impressed with the presentation you gave on your environment research and development program.

9. Are you in the market for a new electrical engineer with a GPA of 3.5 and two years research experience from the University of Northern Colorado?

10. During the Management seminar in Seattle last year, I had the pleasure of hearing you speak on the new business model you have developed. As I have just completed my...

BODY OF LETTER

Your opening paragraph is your introduction and opportunity to present the reader with some immediate and focused information regarding the position you are pursuing and the company you are applying to. Depending on the type of job, you can discuss a few core competencies that demonstrate your strengths.

It's important that you aren't shy at this stage of the letter. It's not bragging to tell the employer what you've done and what you can do. It's up to you to tell potential employers in such a way as to make them take notice. Be bold, honest, and deliberate about listing your qualifications, skills, and accomplishments in this letter.

The second paragraph, often called the sales pitch part of the letter, should highlight your specific qualifications as they apply to this job. Get to the point quickly so the reader can see you are a valuable candidate. Give the details of your skills and education and link them to this position. Use examples to prove that you're a perfect match for the job. If you have specific facts and figures that explain your achievements, then use them. Only put down what you can back up. Remember that a cover letter is also where you include information that isn't on your resume — information that needs to be highlighted as it's pertinent to the job in question.

The third paragraph, sometimes called the flattery paragraph, is where you explain why you have chosen this company. Be sure to research the company so that you can say something positive about them and why you are interested in working for them. Examples of subjects to discuss include research projects they are involved in, their sales records, any awards they may have received, their philosophy or even an article that was written about them.

Regardless of how many letters you are sending out, it is imperative to make sure each one has a personal comment showing you know something about the company.

If necessary you can include another short paragraph to highlight specific experience relating to this job. At the end, summarize what you bring to the job.

There are several ways to approach a cover letter in terms of highlighting job skills. Some professionals believe in a matching list system and others believe in a paragraph highlighting your achievements as they pertain to the necessary qualifications listed in a job ad. Neither is wrong. It's a style and a choice.

For example, here is a short job ad that could be found almost anywhere.

Receptionist position at small busy office. Duties include answering 12-line switchboard, dealing with walk-in customers, making appointments, setting up meetings, ordering supplies, and handling overload of clerical duties when required. Typing and basic computer skills required. Grade 12 graduate. Position to start immediately.

This is a short and simple list of job duties –

- Switchboard
- Customer service
- Setting up meetings
- Ordering supplies
- Typing
- Computer skills

It's okay in a situation where the last couple of skills are heavily interrelated to put them together if space requires. Now look to your own qualifications and pull out what you have for matching skills and put them down in a similar list.

- Four years with 15 line switchboard
- Eight years with customer service experience
- Responsible for ordering supplies monthly
- Four years typing, filing and other clerical duties
- Strong computer skills

You can bullet these or you can put in a sentence that says,

To directly address your required qualifications for this position, I have: (Then put down the list of skills you offer.)

It will look like this:

To address your required qualifications for this position, I have:

- 4 years 15 line switchboard experience
- 8 years customer experience
- Ordered supplies monthly
- 4 years typing, filing and other clerical duties
- Strong computer skills

Some people like to match the list directly by putting up the requirements on one side of the page and then what you offer on the other side of the page, like this:

You asked for — I can offer —

- Switchboard: 4 years 15 line switchboard experience

- Customer service: 8 years customer experience
- Ordering supplies 4 years of being responsible for ordering supplies
- Typing: 4 years typing, filing and other clerical duties
- Computer skills: Strong Microsoft Office and Internet Research skills

You'll notice that in this instance I removed the one qualification that the applicant doesn't have - the one about setting up business meetings. If you don't have experience in this field, then be sure not to give the impression that you do. However, this is something you can easily learn so you have the option of putting it at the end of the list and across in the next column put down minimal experience (if you have any) or put down 'willing to learn,' or leave it off the list altogether. There are many ways to write this list; the important thing is to have something to match to the employer's requirements.

The list look allows the employer to see at glance how you match what they are looking for. If however, they are looking for many different qualifications then it takes a lot of space and above all this letter needs to be succinct. If you can't pull that off then don't match your qualifications in a list form.

Another way to do this is to write out what you offer in a paragraph form. This is shorter and will allow you to discuss more qualifications that you have to offer.

Samples of strong sentences for the body of the cover letter include:

1. Throughout my five years of undergraduate studies, I have learned skills and abilities that are perfect for the position of _____,
2. My experience as a _____ will help me contribute _____ to the position of _____.
3. The highlights of my accomplishments include _____.
4. I am confident that I would be a valuable asset to your organization because _____.
5. My previous experience in _____ has given me valuable experience in _____.
6. As we discussed during the annual Wine Benefit last week, my skills are a particularly good match to the position of _____ with your company _____ because _____.
7. From the position as described, I can tell you right now, I'm the person for the job. My _____ years of experience in _____ have taught me _____ and _____.
8. As the following highlights show, I am well-qualified for the position of _____. I would enjoy an opportunity to discuss the benefits I can offer your organization.
9. It's not often that I see a position that is a direct match to my skills. My experience in _____ is perfect for _____.
10. My last _____ years running _____ has given me a unique skill set that I believe is a perfect match for your position.
11. _____ from the _____ department suggested I contact you regarding the position of _____. We worked together a few years ago for _____ and he feels I would be ideal in this position.
12. My technical skills are excellent and will transfer from _____ department to _____

department easily meaning I'd be up to speed and showing my value immediately. I'd love an opportunity to discuss this further.

13. The last two years I managed an office staff of _____. Even through cutbacks and the economic slump, I managed to keep on budget with the company moving forward in a viable way.

THE CLOSING PARAGRAPH

The closing paragraph is to tie your interest to the position, thank the employer, provide the necessary contact information, and indicate the follow-up action you are planning to take. It's common to state what you'd like to consider the next step, such as him contacting you to discuss your application or you calling as a follow up on your application. It's important that if you say you are going to call them that you do so.

When considering your next step, realize there are several ways to end the letter. You can have a call to action or a no call to action type of close. What does this mean? As your purpose of writing this cover letter is to motivate the employer to bring you in for that all-important interview, you want to end with someone doing something toward making this happen. That often means ending with an action, such as you telling the employer that you will call to set up a time for an interview.

Be confident and state that you will call next Friday if you don't hear before then. You can also change that slightly to: I will call you at the end of next week to discuss my qualifications for this position. If this time frame doesn't work for you, feel free to contact me at (phone number or email) before then.

Other examples include:

1. I'll call your office next week to determine a convenient time to discuss your specific needs and my qualifications.

2. I'll contact you next week to discuss this job or other opportunities where my skills and qualifications are suited.

3. Early next week, I'll email you to set up a time to discuss this position and my experience.

4. There are many ways that I can already see to increasing your company's sales. It's something we could explore together. I'll call you early next week to set up a time.

5. My resume is only part of the story. Why don't we meet to discuss my qualifications and your job requirements further? I'll call you early next week to confirm a date.

If you aren't comfortable calling the employer then you need to close in such a way that they know you will be waiting to hear back. This is a more standard closing but that doesn't make it the right one for everyone

A sample of this type of standard, but also weaker closing goes like this:

1. I've attached a copy of my resume for your consideration. I look forward to hearing from you.

2. Enclosed, please find a copy of my resume. If you feel that I have what you are looking for, then please call me at (phone number and/or email).

3. Thank you for your time and consideration. Please call at your earliest convenience.

4. I am eager to learn more about _____ and would appreciate an opportunity to discuss my qualifications and interests with you.

5. I am interested in the position and would appreciate an opportunity to discuss my background as it pertains to your requirements further.

6. I feel that my _____ and _____ make me a strong candidate for this position and would appreciate an opportunity to discuss this further.

CLOSING

There are some standard phrases that seem to end up on every letter. If you want to stand out, anything that you can do to make yourself unique, while still being professional, is good. The following closings will do, but they are weak:

1. Thank you for your time and consideration.

2. Sincerely,

3. Very truly yours,

4. Best wishes,

You can also show a little personality here if you wish. Consider the following choices:

1. Best wishes, always,

2. With confidence,

3. Enthusiastically,

4. Warmest,

5. Until next week,

SENDING A LETTER

Mailing a letter has not gone out of style, although email is certainly the most popular way to correspond. Many times, you are required to mail your cover letter and resume. Use a standard white business envelope when mailing. Please don't allow your personality to show at this stage. Purple envelopes with butterfly stickers are not going to give the right impression to the employer.

As a general rule, print the name and address of the employer on the front of the envelope. There are two different opinions on putting a return address on the envelope. The general consensus is to put down a return address and if the letter goes awry then you will get the letter back again – in theory. The other line of thought says that most people open a white business letter without a return address because they don't know what's in it.

Another consideration is if you want a reply and aren't sure if you will get one or not, make it easy on the employer. Tuck a stamped and addressed card or a return envelope inside with your letter as a convenience. This is likely to increase your response rate. Many people today think that they can email everything and in some cases you can. But not always and when you have to mail in your resume and cover letter, why not make it easy on the employer to respond.

Don't put anything else on the envelope except the person's name, company and the company address. Do not write, 'Resume inside' or 'Personal and confidential' on the outside and never go so far as to say, 'The solution to all your problems lies inside.' That's liable to get your application tossed into the garbage unopened.

ADDRESSING SALARY ISSUES

It's awkward trying to address the issue of salary when you will have a limited understanding of the duties and responsibilities of the position in question. So it seems foolish to give an expected salary when you don't have all the information. However, many employers ask for just that in a job posting.

The rule is if you're not asked then don't volunteer any information on salary expectations or salary history.

Some ads will ask you to provide salary history or salary requirements when you submit your application. This is telling you that the company has a fixed budget for this position and salary requirements are likely to be an issue in selecting the person who is eventually hired. There could still be some flexibility in this budget, but it's not likely to be much.

If you are going to address this issue it always goes in the last paragraph of the cover letter.

There are differences between Salary Expectations and Salary History.

SALARY EXPECTATION

If a job posting asks for this information, they want to know what salary you would want to do the job in question.

First off, only address this question if the requirement is explicit in the job ad as this knowledge obviously gives the hiring manager a distinct advantage. Address this topic only if the ad states something similar to **"only submissions providing salary (history) will be considered."**

If it's stated in the ad there are several options:

1. The first is to ignore the request and try to build as strong a case as possible with your accomplishments and skills to prove you are the best person for the job. If you have what the employer is looking for, he may call you or bring you in for an interview. Or he may cull your resume from the pile and toss it in the garbage because you haven't put down what he's specified.

2. You can make the hiring manager aware that the information is available, but only further down the process, such as 'Full salary history will be made available during the interview.'

3. Another option is to sidestep the issue and say something like, 'Salary is negotiable.'

4. This option is to give a range of salary that you are looking for from the minimum you would be willing to accept to the highest you would expect to be paid. **My salary requirement is in the mid to high fifty range. If you would like further details please contact me at _____.**

The problem with giving a salary range, is that it can limit your chance to negotiate a higher wage. As you already don't know what the responsibilities of the position are, you don't want to lose the advantage of getting a higher salary later.

You also need to know an average salary range for a similar position. That means doing wage research before answering the ad. You can ask recruiters, other hiring managers, the local librarians, and search online to find salary information.

Here are a few places to look: Add in full website

1.PayScale - Salary survey, salaries, wages, compensation information, and analysis. Includes evaluations for job offers or raises, and salary in your current position.

2.The Occupational Outlook Handbook - statistics on that targeted position or potential career path, including educational requirements, national salary levels, working environment, and more.

3.National Association of Realtors® Salary Calculator - Calculates cost of living factors by location and salary.

4.Salary Surveys by JobStar – salary guides for positions.

SALARY HISTORY

Only offer this information if it is requested in the ad. Why would a potential employer want this information? It helps him to weed out candidates that 'appear' to be over or under qualified and it gives him an advantage at the negotiation stage.

If your salary history is well below the budget for that position, he may think you are under qualified and drop the budget to save money on your hire. If you put down a salary history that is way higher than their budget, he may feel that you are over qualified and that they can't afford to hire you.

Normally, you would give a separate sheet of information with the information requested in reverse chronological order, similar to your resume, listing the position you held, the company name, time you worked there, and your salary. Alternatively, you put down the starting and ending salary to show your growth with the company.

Your sheet will look similar to this.

SALARY HISTORY

Manager

Tallahassee Corporation, Tallahassee, FL

Feb. 2002 - June 2008

Annual Salary: $58,000

Or

Manager

Tallahassee Corporation, Tallahassee, FL

Feb. 2002 - June 2008

Starting Salary: $35,000 (add in benefits)

Ending Salary: $58,000 (add in benefits)

You do need to add in all benefits and bonuses that you received along with your salary.

4. EMAILING VS MAILING

Ten years ago, there wouldn't have been a question over how to send a cover letter but times have changed and this is a question everyone is facing today. There's no doubt that email is faster, cheaper, and easier for the sender, but the truth is in the attitude of the person you are contacting.

If you don't know what this person's preference is, and you have no way to find out, then the safest thing to do is to mail a standard letter and give your email address as part of your contact information. If you've had correspondence with the hiring manager already, then continue with the same form of communication – if the instructions don't tell you to do something different. Follow all instructions implicitly. Don't guess. If you are in doubt about something they have said, ask. It's also possible they will ask you to forward your application to someone else. The bottom line here is to READ the correspondence carefully.

Be sure to check the company's website for this type of information as it is usually listed. If an email address is there as a contact, then use it.

If there is no email contact then you are better off sending a letter by mail.

It's also a huge mistake to take a random person's email address, often found on the website or through an article, and ask that stranger to send your application to the right person. Don't do this. It's bad form, unprofessional, and will only get your application deleted. If you are determined to send an email, then phone the department and ask for the correct email address of the person you want to contact.

If this is someone in the Human Resources department, the reception will also have instructions as to releasing this email to people. If you do get the address, please confirm the spelling of the person's name.

WHAT CAN YOU SEND VIA EMAIL?

Most correspondence can be done by email in today's age of electronic communication. It's fine to email your thank you notes after an interview has taken place. A mailed letter is still a nice touch though so don't discount this method. If however, a hiring decision is going to be made very soon, as in the next day or two, email allows you to get that polite note of appreciation in before the decision and just might turn the tide in your favor.

If you've had a phone conversation where details were discussed then it's very helpful to put those into an email as written confirmation. If you agreed verbally to an interview date then an email is a great way to confirm and follow up.

This is particularly important if you've been offered a job over the phone. Either ask to have the details confirmed in writing while speaking to the person who has just offered you the job, or send one yourself so that the details are clearly understood.

It is common for an employer to confirm an offer in writing, but many small companies don't have a person designated to handle the hiring details. In this case, a written follow up on the offer could be overlooked.

Should you be confirming a job offer and still have questions, you can still send an email, but chances are good that a phone call is the better way to go. If you can't reach anyone over the phone, then do send the email and request that they contact you as you still have a few questions.

If you need to negotiate or if the terms aren't as you understood them to be, then do try to call first. Again, if you can't reach anyone, then email and let them know you have questions that you need answers to and you'd like to speak with someone directly. Negotiations are always better in person, then over the phone, and last in writing. Once the negotiations are completed, be sure to get the terms down in writing.

THE DIFFERENCE BETWEEN THE BASIC PIECES

A standard letter is discussed in great detail as we move forward in this book, but there are few differences in the structure of an email letter versus the standard letter.

THE SUBJECT LINE

If you are replying to an email, don't change the subject line. Hit reply, answer the email using proper English, and send it off. Don't delete the original message; the person receiving this new email can see at a glance the thread of the conversation. If the email is full of irrelevant material than cut those parts out but leave the essence of what you are responding to for the person to see what they originally sent you.

If this is a new conversation, be sure to put a clear, concise message in the subject line. If you've been given a job posting number then put that in the subject line. If this is a follow up email to confirm an appointment then say so. If this is a follow up email to confirm details of a phone conversation then put that in the subject line.

Don't leave the subject line blank and don't put in something like, 'Please look at my application.' Instead re-word it to – 'Application for job posting F578'.

There is a trend to putting statements like 'for your consideration," or 'for your information' on the subject line. This is an empty type of message. An email means you are initiating contact for some reason to begin with so clarify why. Don't waste the employer's time.

THE DATE

The date in a standard letter goes between your return address and the address of the person you are contacting.

In an email, the date will automatically show up on the person's email program so it's not required in the body of the email. You can put it down if it makes you uncomfortable not to but it is not required.

YOUR EMAIL ADDRESS

You email address will also automatically show up in the other person's email program and is therefore not something you put on your email. It is however, a good idea to include your email in your signature block as discussed under that section. This is also where we tend to not see a potential problem.

Hopefully, you did this prior to writing your resume and cover letter, but it's important to have a professional looking email address. Many people don't consider the long-term consequences when they first create their main email address with names that will get them deleted or caught in spam with their application never making it to the person's inbox. When you're sixteen, having an email that reads bieberforever@hotmail.com might work, but being now eighteen and looking for a job, it isn't.

The number of people who have emails like nuttinbetter@yahoo.com or missyfrenchy@global.net are huge. Don't be one of them if you expect to be treated as a professional.

Instead, get a plain email, preferably with your full name and leave the other email to use with your friends.

MAILING ADDRESSES

In a standard business letter, you start with your name and your return address, including street, followed by the city, state and the ZIP code on the following line. Be sure to have your email address below that.

In an email, your return address isn't required. You can include it if you choose, but it's not standard in a formal style email. You can add this information after your name at the very bottom of the letter in your signature block if you choose. They will have your contact information from receiving the email. They can hit reply and follow up.

In a standard letter, the next set of addresses is the recipient's full name, title, company name, company street address and then the city, state and ZIP code. This is often followed by the phone number if you know it.

When it comes to email format, there is a division over whether this second address is required. It's more formal and more professional to have it there than it is to remove it. If the email is to be of a more casual tone, then you can start the email directly with the salutation. In all other cases, it's better to err on the side of caution and put the address information in.

SALUTATIONS ON AN EMAIL LETTER

In a standard business letter, you always use a formal salutation such as Dear Mr. or Ms., followed by the person's last name. That is no different with an email letter.

YOUR SIGNATURE

In a standard letter format, you would put in your closing salutation, 'Warmest' or 'Sincerely yours,' and then leave several lines and type your full name. Before mailing the letter, you would sign the letter.

In an email, we have the signature block to deal with. There is no handwritten signature in an email although you could add one in a graphic, but that could cause problems as well. There is, however, a series of lines that create the block of information after your name called a signature block.

Don't make your signature block longer than four lines if possible. Include your name, contact information, email address, and phone number. Some people like to include graphics or sayings as part of their signature block, but in this case it is best not to. Graphics may not load properly, take too long to download, and what is a nice saying to you may be offensive to someone else.

LETTER STYLE

There is a tendency to make emails less formal in form and style and this ends up being dangerous with job applications. You always want to give a professional appearance. That means using proper business language and excellent grammar skills in a clear and easy to read way. This is exactly the same for any type of business letter whether it goes via email or in a standard letter format.

Make sure you proofread this document like you would any other. The content layout is the same as for the standard letter and is discussed at length in the rest of this book.

Only use standard fonts, no fancy scripts or fonts, write in normal upper and lower case and not blocked caps, as this infers shouting. Also keep the fonts to a normal size instead of very large writing. The people you are emailing will be expecting normal business communication style and being different in this case is not a good thing.

Be sure to use proper words, not shortened text words that are often used when communicating by cell phones and do use proper grammar and punctuation.

Another thing to consider is the color of your letters, the page, and decorations. At the risk of sounding repetitive, don't. This is business and that means standard, plain white background, and standard black font without any decorative touches.

This word of caution also applies to the use of graphics. Don't. Not in this type of communication. Many people like to use a graphic as part of their signature block. This can cause a problem for the recipient of the email. It can be taken as a virus and could be caught up in a spam filter.

ATTACHMENTS

When it comes to attachments read your instructions carefully and only send an attachment if requested. Often, you are asked to send both a cover letter and resume as attachments. That means you write up a standard cover letter and attach it. In this case, you write a short email explaining what you have attached and why. Do not send a blank email. Be sure to write this email in a concise and businesslike way.

Example of an Email with attachments:

Subject: Web Designer position

Dear Mr. Watson,

Please find attached my application for the Web Designer position advertised on your website. I have attached my resume and cover letter.

Should you require any further information, please contact me on my cell phone at (333) 444-5555.

Thank you for considering my application.

Sincerely,

Jane Smith

Other employers may want only the resume attached. Still other people won't deal with attachments and will instruct you to paste your resume into the body of the email.

When attaching the required documents, consider how the names you've used to save your document look. Are they intuitive for the other person to understand or were they saved in some kind of code that only you know? The general rule is to save the document as firstnamelastnameresume.doc (or .rtf if they have requested this format). You want the recipient of this resume to see at a glance what they have been sent and by whom. Some people might request a specific format, such as NOT .docx but .doc or .rtf and even .pdf might be encouraged. Be sure to send an allowable format otherwise the other person won't be able to open the document.

GOOD BUSINESS PRACTICES

Remember to be professional and polite in your communications. This is a written record of what you say and if you say something wrong, it can come back to haunt you, so watch the tone of your words. If the email is important, print off a copy of what you've sent and all communications that you've received. Particularly if there are any communications regarding finances and benefits, for example. You want to have proof of what was said and when it was said in case there's a problem in the future.

TIMING

When you receive some type of communication from the hiring manager, be sure to respond promptly. If you delay answering, you could make him think that you aren't interested.

However, when you are waiting to hear from the hiring manager, realize that they will take however long they need before getting back to you. In many cases, you may never hear anything. That is the downfall of the Internet right now. It makes jobs very accessible to so many people that recruiters and managers are often overwhelmed with applicants. Just to maintain sanity, they will only contact those who they are interested in speaking with further.

Regardless of the type of communication, it's polite to answer. If the email is telling you that you have NOT been selected for an interview, or second interview etc, still respond with a polite thank you. These people have given you their time and attention and it's important to respond in kind.

THE BIGGEST MISTAKES WHEN EMAILING
COVER LETTERS

Almost everyone uses email, particularly if you live in the Western world. Most communication is done this way, and yet people consistently make the same mistakes.

When it comes to sending cover letters, it's even more important that you:

1. Don't overlook the importance of the subject line. It's a tool that can make or break your delivery. Never send a blank subject line. Make the subject line a hook that starts your application. Consider a busy employer who opens his email and a hundred emails download to his computer. Yours needs to stand out from the others without wasting the employer's time. Make it count.

2. Don't forget to personalize and address the email properly. Don't use first names when you address an employer. Email is already an informal communication style, but you don't want to make it seem like you know this person personally. 'Dear Sir' also sounds like you don't know or care who you are sending your application to. Address the person by name.

3. Don't write long, tedious emails. Keep your communication short and to the point. Email messages are supposed to be short. So don't make your email longer than a few sentences if you are attaching your cover letter and only a few paragraphs if the email is your cover letter.

4. Don't forget how sharp your words can sound when delivered in an email. Don't write words in block capitals in order to get your point across. Avoid colored fonts for the same reason.

5. Don't forget to use proper business spelling and not allowing your casual style to dominate. Using the short form of R in place of 'are' is not acceptable. Email is casual, but not that casual.

6. Don't forget that any response you get from the employer is private and confidential. You don't have the right to forward it to anyone else. People often forget and forward it on to a friend to read. Don't. It's not professional. That also means don't say anything that you wouldn't want someone else to see in your email. You don't know where it might end up.

7. Don't forget your contact information. Often people write a nice business style email, and forget about their signature. Are you utilizing your signature block correctly? Create a signature block with your contact information, such as your phone number, fax number and even your mailing address. This helps an employer to find you without having to search around for the information.

8. Don't 'bold' your entire email. Nor should you set the font too large. People can read the 'normal' font just fine.

9. Don't be impatient. If you'd mailed a letter, you know you'd have to wait weeks for a response. Email in business can take just as long. Don't email the person every day looking for a response. If you need a response, then call the person – don't fill his inbox with lots of irritating emails.

The rule of thumb for email communication is that if you wouldn't do it in a proper business letter, then don't do it in any email communication.

EMAIL COVER LETTER FORMAT — INFORMAL

Subject line – job position or reference number

Dear Mr./Ms. (last name),

In the body, let the employer know what you have to offer and why you are the right person for the position.

Include at the beginning why you are writing, how you found the position and mention if you were referred by a mutual friend.

Next, clearly describe what you have to offer the employer. Match the job requirements to your qualifications. Be specific and mention how your accomplishments are a perfect match to the position.

In the last paragraph, mention if you are attaching your resume then conclude with an action close and an appreciation for the person considering you for the position.

Close with something like 'Best Regards,'

Finish with your name,
Address
Email
Phone

5.COLD CONTACT LETTER

This type of letter is also known as a first contact letter, inquiry, introductory, or broadcast letter. Realize that only about 25% of all jobs are advertised, making the other 75% ones that you need to find on your own.

Use this letter to contact a company that hasn't placed a job add and that may or may not have any openings. You are using the letter as an introduction of your skills and resume hoping that the person who reads it on the other end is the hiring manager or knows who to forward the letter to.

This type of letter can spark an interest and lead to further contact. Results can be difficult though, as you don't know if the company hires people with your skill set or are strapped financially; don't be upset if you receive only a few responses.

You need to research the target companies before writing the letter so that you can narrow your list to companies with the highest potential of responding. To avoid wasting everyone's time, make sure your type of skills are required at this company. It's easy to say that every company needs a marketing professional, but keep in mind that many companies have started outsourcing specific departments and if your field is one they outsource, you are wasting everyone's time. One way to find out is to pick up the phone and contact the office. A few simple questions will help you to define your list.

As this is more of a fishing expedition, leave off the formal tone and try to be more conversational. You still need to give every sentence a good review to make sure it is as strong as possible.

Also remember that you are not the only person sending out this type of letter. Therefore try to make yours personal and unique.

WHAT GOES IN THE COLD CONTACT LETTER?

This type of letter should contain, along with the standard letter parts, clear information as to:

- Why you've contacted the company.
- Why the company interests you.
- Why your skills and accomplishments should be of interest to the company.
- What follow-up you are going to do.

SAMPLE 1 — COLD CALL LETTER VIA EMAIL

Remember, a more formal email uses the full address of both the sender and the recipient. In this sample there is only one address for the recipient.

Mr. Schwartz
Development Manager
Success Canada,
123 Main Street,
Vancouver, BC
VON 1V6

Dear Mr. Schwartz,
A project like Success Canada requires an organized, efficient, and hardworking Administrator to ensure that every day goes smoothly. My administrative experience can help make Success Canada the long enduring benefit program it is meant to be.

I have ten years of administrative experience with non-profit organizations, having helped grow Children's Network to the international success it is today. Over the last decade, I have contributed to the many decision-making processes while keeping the day-to-day activities operating smoothly as the company grew from 10 to 32 employees. Prior to that, I worked in the education system as an academic administrator.

My resume is attached. I'd love a chance to speak with you further to discuss the ways in which I can help grow your organization. I'll call you next week to arrange a time for an interview.

I appreciate your time.

Sincerely,

Jane Smith
123 Address Drive
Jobless, CA 95255
Jsmith@email.com
Cell: 123-444-5555

SAMPLE 2 — COLD CALL LETTER TO MAIL

Jane Smith
123 Address Drive
Jobless, CA 95255
jsmith@email.com
Cell: 123—444—5555

January 10, 2011

John Doe
HR Manager
Corporation Unknown
345 Main Street
Jobless, CA 95255

Dear Mr. Doe,

I am looking to join a company that enjoys enthusiastic employees who excel at customer service with which I can expand my career in event planning.

My attached resume will show you an overview of my 10 years of experience in event planning for Chatham Inc. My years of customer experience, organizational skills, and planning on deadlines have given me a unique insight into this industry and I would love to build on my achievements.

I'm passionate about this industry and I'm looking for an opportunity to plan some of the large events that your company handles, such as the International Wine and Cheese Competition, the annual Computer Expo event, and Crankworks. This is my area of expertise and I know that I would be an asset to your company.

If you need further information, feel free to contact me. Otherwise, I will call you early next week to discuss this matter further. Thank you for your consideration.

Best wishes,

Jane Smith
Enclosure

6. THE APPLICATION LETTER

This is the letter most people refer to as a 'cover letter.'

It is an 'application' letter used to apply for a specific job and always goes with your resume. As the first thing that the hiring manager will see, it needs to connect you, your skills, and experience to the job opening.

WHAT GOES IN THE APPLICATION LETTER?

Besides your full contact information, correct name, and address of the person you are contacting, remember to explain why you are contacting this person, and to use your best sales pitch to interest the reader into looking at your resume.

All the detailed information in Chapter 3 applies specifically to this type of letter so reread if necessary.

The core elements include:

- Relate your individual skills and accomplishments to those that are listed in the job posting. If the company has listed a skill, it's because they need it or a reasonable substitute. Show that you have what they need.

- Highlight the way in which you can benefit the company. Remember to keep the company's needs in your mind as you write this. They have a problem and you want them to see you as the solution. Give them what they ask for.

- Use facts, figures, and accomplishments that are real and tangible. Never inflate your past results as they might check. Refer to the other sections in this book to make the letter as tight and as powerful as possible.

- If you don't have much in experience, highlight any volunteer work or pull from any extracurricular activities to support why you are the right person for the job.

- Don't forget to reference your resume in the letter and add enclosure at the bottom of the page so they see that you have included your resume. If you are sending the resume by email, utilize the subject line of the email to clearly state the position you are applying for.

Let's review how the letter should look.

SAMPLE 1 — FORM LETTER FOR MAILING

Full Name
Address
City, State, ZIP

Date

Employer Name
Title
Company Name
Company address
City, State, ZIP

Dear Mr./Ms. (Last name of contact):

This opening paragraph says why you are writing to this person, how you learned about the position and refers to the position title as used by the employer.

The second paragraph should highlight your specific qualifications as it applies to this job. Give details of your skills and education and link them to this position to show that you should be considered for an interview. You need to use examples to show that you have the necessary skills for the job.

This is the paragraph that goes into further qualifications and skills if necessary and needs to discuss why you have chosen this company.

The closing paragraph is to tie your interest to the position, thank the employer, provide the necessary contact information, and indicate the follow— up action you are planning to take. It's common to state what you'd like to consider the next step, such as being contacted to discuss your application or you calling as a follow up on your application. It's important that if you say you are going call that you do so.

Always close with something like Best wishes or Warmest,

Signature

Your name
Enclosures

SAMPLE 2 — COVER LETTER

Dante Slocum
123 Who Knew Street
Portland, OR 97208
dslocum@email.com
(333)—444—5555

November 4, 2011

Mr. John Rogers
Northgate Recreation Center
4332 Adelaide Drive

Portland, OR 97208

Dear Mr. Rogers:

With the opening of the new complex, you will be needing people with great organization and administrative experience. I am one of those people and am very interested in joining your team in an administrative capacity on this exciting new venture.

My administrative experience includes 8 years in the recreation field, a complement to my diploma in Recreation and Tourism, which focused on creating suitable programs for the public. Years of developing age and skill appropriate programs to a diverse community has given me excellent experience in customer service, public relations, and maintaining a budget.

I know I would be an asset to your team and would love an opportunity to speak further with you. I'll contact you early next week to discuss the matter further. Should you need any information prior to this time, feel free to call or email me.

Thank you for your consideration.

Sincerely,

Dante Slocum
Encl.

7. THE REFERRAL LETTER

This type of letter is also referred to as a sponsor letter.

A referral letter is one of the best ways to open doors to new leads. It means that you've been generally referred to the company by someone at the company or knowledgeable of the company and the industry. These can often come from informational interviews and this person's name was passed on as the next place to contact.

WHAT GOES IN THE REFERRAL LETTER?

This type of letter requires you to:

- Address the letter to a specific person and be sure to find and use his/her title correctly.
- Mention the person who referred you to the company within the body of your letter and preferably close to the beginning. Remember to spell his/her name and title properly.

- Be clear about your reason for contacting this person.
- If you know him/her, explain where you both met and what might have been discussed previously.
- Put in your qualifications, skills, and accomplishments, but keep it brief as you want to keep focused.
- In the last paragraph, have a statement to influence the action you'd like the hiring manager to take.
- Always close with an action statement such as stating when you will contact them.

SAMPLE 1 — REFERRAL LETTER

Jane Smith
123 Main Street
Portland, OR 97208
jsmith@email.com
(333) 444 5555

June 12, 2011

Mr. David Homer,
VP Sales and Marketing
Cansas Corp.
456 Downtown Ave
Portland, OR 97283

Dear Mr. Homer:

I spoke with John Sprott from your Seattle office last week and he recommended that I contact you regarding the new business model you have implemented in your department and the position you've taken with social media.

My 10 years of experience has been in public relations for Danfor Corp. In the last several years, I initiated several social media avenues for the company in order to increase the company profile. A few of these avenues included developing newsletters through the newly designed website, and increasing and interacting with followers on LinkedIn, Facebook, and even Twitter.

The work was rewarding and I enjoyed connecting with the many different people. I am interested in finding a position with similar opportunities. Please take the time to review my resume as I believe I would be an asset to your company.

I will call you early next week to set up a convenient time to discuss this further. I appreciate your consideration in this matter.

Best wishes,

Jane Smith

Enclosure

SAMPLE 2 — REFERRAL LETTER

Name
Address
City, State, ZIP
Phone
Email

Date

Name
Title
Company
Address
City, State, ZIP

Dear Mr./Ms.(Last name):

I am contacting you to express interest in the Quality Control department at Gendo Inc. I am very familiar with the biochemical industry and the types of research your company is working on. My old colleague, Jane Doe, has recommended that I contact you directly about this position. Jane and I worked together in the Quality Control department of Biozyme for five years. She felt I would be a good match for Gendo.

I spent five years in QC at Chemcom before accepting a supervisory position in Biozyme. We managed QC for four departments and 44 scientists and technicians.

Please take the opportunity to review my resume. I believe I would be a great asset to your company. I'd appreciate an opportunity to meet with you and discuss an opportunity to work at Gendo Inc. further. Thank you for your consideration in this matter.

Best regards,

Jenny Cochrane
Enclosure

8. THE NETWORKING LETTER

 networking letter is similar to a referral letter, only you're requesting information from someone regarding an industry or other business information.

As networking is an important tool for finding a job, it's important to contact everyone you know to open up any job opportunities.

WHAT GOES IN A NETWORKING LETTER?

The elements between this and a referral letter are similar but have a couple of differences.

Be sure to:

- Address to a specific person.
- State how you know this person and why you are contacting him.
- Tell where you met and what you discussed.

- Include your qualifications, skills, accomplishments, but keep it brief as you want to focus on the information you are seeking.

- You can ask for information on job leads, an introduction to other contacts, or anything else that may help you in your job search.

- In the last paragraph have a statement to influence the action you'd like the person to take.

- Close with an action statement.

SAMPLE 1 — NETWORKING LETTER CASUAL EMAIL INFORMAL

Dear Mr. Hartford,

A mutual friend, Jenny Lee, encouraged me to send my resume to you. I've known Jenny for years through our degree program and our extracurricular activities. Jenny mentioned that she has really enjoyed working the type of work she's done for your company.

I am interested in getting a job in horticulture while I'm off for the summer. I am a Botany student and have worked at the local botanical gardens prior to starting my full time studies.

I would appreciate any recommendations you can offer in regards to my job search. I appreciate your consideration in this matter and look forward to hearing from you.

Best regards,

Jane Smith

SAMPLE 2 — NETWORKING LETTER

Contact
Name
Title
Company
Address
City, State, ZIP

Dear Mr./Ms. (Last name):

I was referred to you by _____ from _____ in _____. She stated that you were an excellent source on the latest research and development work in the medical devices field.

My goal is to secure a mid-level sales position in this industry. I would appreciate hearing any advice you can offer on career opportunities in your company and in the industry. I am new to this city but have settled in and am eager to go to work.

Thank you so much for your consideration and any insight and advice you're willing to offer. I'll contact you early next week to set up a time to discuss this matter further.

Best regards,

Jane Smith
Enclosures

9. PROSPECTING LETTER

L etters of this type are sent out to organizations when asking about possible job vacancies and even a request for an informational interview.

The body of this letter has a similar layout as the application letter. You want to be sure to list your qualifications in order of relevance to have the hiring manager consider you for the job in question.

It's a good idea to follow this type of letter with a follow up phone call. It's quite likely you won't receive any response to your letter otherwise.

Be sure to give a time frame in which you will be contacting this person. Be generous with the time as well, and set a date at least five days ahead. Be sure to follow through on the phone call. Give the person sufficient time to get your letter, read it, and evaluate it before you follow up.

WHAT GOES IN A PROSPECTING LETTER?

Elements to consider in this type of letter include:

- Be sure to find and use the correct name and title for the person you are contacting.
- In the first paragraph, put down why you are contacting the company, how you heard about the position, why the company is of interest, and if you have researched the company.
- In the second and possibly third paragraphs, introduce yourself and discuss the highlights of your qualifications and education. Only list significant achievements as you are going to send a resume along with the letter. Also provide any information that is not on your resume. As you aren't responding to a job ad, you can't match your skills to a specific set of requirements. However, it is important to give as detailed a listing of what skills you can offer.
- In the last paragraph, state that you will call to set up a time for an appointment. It's important to thank the person and show some eagerness about an upcoming meeting.

The next few pages are sample prospecting letters. Go ahead and fill in the blanks so you have the right information where you need it, then rewrite so it's not a carbon copy.

All four samples are in the standard mailing format. Two are for students looking for work. Follow the instructions in the Emailing vs Mailing section to adapt to email format. In general, just remove the top of the letter and start with the address for a more informal email style.

SAMPLE 1 — FORM PROSPECTING LETTER

Your name
Your address
City, State, ZIP
Your email

Date

Contact's name
Title
Company name
Company address
City, State, ZIP

Dear Mr./Ms. (Last name),

Through a friend, (name of friend and title if applicable), from (company name), I have learned of a potential job opening in my field. After further research into the company, its credentials, and policies, I'd like to express an interest in working with (company name) as (title) where I believe I could make a difference. Some of my credentials include a degree in (name degree and any majors that pertain to the type of position you are looking to find) from (name institute). (Name the highlights of your career achievements in two or three sentences.)

I believe my knowledge and understanding of (list your areas of specialty here as they pertain to the job you are applying for), together with my (list other skills like communication, management etc.) will make me an excellent candidate for this position in your organization. Please find enclosed a copy of my resume. I'd appreciate a chance to discuss my skills and education with you further. I will call you early next week to set up a potential time. Thank you for your consideration.

Sincerely,

Signature
Your name
Encl.

SAMPLE 2 — FOR A POTENTIAL JOB

Your name
Your address
City, State, ZIP
Your email

Date

Contact's name
Title
Company name
Company address
City, State, ZIP

Dear Mr./Ms. (Last name),

After reading about your company in the (name a place you've heard about the company), and hearing about the work you are doing on (name something about the type of work the company is doing), I decided to approach you regarding the possibility of a job opening. I am interested in working in the (name your area of interest) field.

My education includes (list a degree or the highlights of your education) from (name the institute where you were educated). I have experience in (name field) from working at (name company). As well, I have worked (name other experience that pertains to the type of job you are looking for).

I'm enclosing my resume and would appreciate an opportunity to discuss potential job openings available at your company. I can be reached through my email (list your email address) and by phone at (list your number.)

Thank you for reviewing my resume. I look forward to hearing from you.

Sincerely,

Signature
Your name
Enclosure

FOR STUDENTS

This type of letter is of greater importance for students as they sometimes need to contact companies looking for positions. Therefore, I have included sample letters specifically for students to use.

The first sample explains what goes into each paragraph and how to present the information.

There are two samples. The first is for all students, while the second one is for graduating students looking to launch into their new careers.

SAMPLE 3 — FORM LETTER FOR STUDENTS

Your name
Address
City, State, ZIP
Email address

Date

Contact's name
Title
Company name
Address
City, State, ZIP

Dear Mr./Ms. (Name),

First Paragraph – *Right at the beginning, introduce yourself and list your degree program and the year you will graduate. State if you are looking for a full-time or a summer position. Explain why you are writing, name the title of the position you are looking for, or field and general industry in which you are interested. Explain where you heard about the position and if you were referred by someone; be sure to include that information.*

Second Paragraph: Here is where you mention your qualifications, skills learned and accomplishments. List what you think would be of greatest interest. Be sure to state why you want to work for the company, location, or type of work. Highlight any related training and experience. State that you have enclosed (attached) a resume.

Third Paragraph: Finish the letter with an action close that clearly states what you are going to do. State that you will phone or email in a week and try to be as specific as possible. If you say you're going to phone, then be sure to follow through.

Include a phone number and email where you may be reached.

Sincerely,

Signature

Applicant Name
Encl. (Only include this if mailing a letter)

SAMPLE 4 — FORM LETTER FOR GRADUATING STUDENTS

Your name
Your address
City, State, ZIP
Your email

Date

Name
Title
Company name
Company address
City, State, ZIP

Dear Mr./Ms. (Last name),
After conducting extensive research, I was impressed with what I read regarding (name of company) and its (put down something you found out about the company through your research).

In (give month of completing studies), I will be graduating from (give College or University) with my (name degree or finished level) in (name specialty). I am interested in (name area that you are hoping to become employed in) with a specialty in (name an area of interest that applies to your field). I am hoping to work on this career path after my graduation.

I'm enclosing a copy of my resume, showing my educational background and my work experience in (list your experience that is pertinent to the type of position you are hoping to get). Besides this experience I also worked as (list other work experience) at (list company name where you worked) in (list location of the company). I would appreciate an opportunity to discuss the possibility of employment with (name the company) and will call next week to follow up.

Please feel free to contact me at (give email and phone number).

Warmest,

Signature

Grant Summers
Enclosures

10. FOLLOW UP LETTERS

This is a follow-up letter after an interview. Many people think this type of letter is not required and they couldn't be more wrong. This type of letter is essential. Not only is it proper manners, and good business practice, but it further builds on the rapport with the interviewer. You need to thank that person for the time they spent considering your application. Should an additional job come up, you want the interviewer to remember you. A thank you letter goes a long way to doing just that.

It's not just good manners, it's a way to help the hiring manager remember you and your qualifications. You may have had one interview that day, but a hiring manager could easily have sat through a dozen. They can't be expected to remember the details unique to each person. Yes, they will have a file and notes that they took during each session or right afterwards, however, several days can go by and they've moved on to interviewing other candidates for an unrelated position.

Sending a thank you letter helps this manager to place you at the top of his or her mind again. It's another marketing tool in an economic situation where thousands of people are applying for the same position. It's also something the manager will appreciate, leaving her with a good impression of you.

Should the candidates have been narrowed down to just a couple of people, and the employer is having trouble deciding between them, a pleasant, well—written thank you letter could make all the difference.

WHAT GOES INTO THE FOLLOW—UP LETTER?

Thank you letters need to be accurate and polite. Be sure to spell the person's name correctly. If you saw more than one person then be sure to send a thank you letter to every person you saw.

Be sure to make a short statement about your qualifications and restate your interest in the position.

In general:

- The first paragraph should express your appreciation for the interview, state the job you were interviewed for and give date and location of the interview.

- The second paragraph should reiterate your interest in the job and emphasize the match between your qualifications and the job requirements.

- The third paragraph should add any new or clarifying details that you want to add now that you've had time to think about the interview.

This type of letter can be either handwritten and mailed or, given today's communication system, emailed. If you are hand writing it, make sure your printing/writing is clear and legible and written on good paper.

If your interview was extremely formal, it is better to type a thank you letter and to mail it in.

WHEN DO YOU SEND THE LETTER?

The best advice is to send it within 48 hours of your interview. Make sure you keep it short, just two to three short paragraphs, and be professional. Do not ask for the job! Instead make an enthusiastic case for you being the right candidate for this great job.

SAMPLE 1 — STANDARD FOLLOW UP LETTER

Your name
Your address
City, State, ZIP
Email address

Date

Contact's name
Title
Company name
Address
City, State, ZIP

Dear Mr./Ms. (Last name),

Thank you for taking the time to go over the (position) job at (Company name) with me. I was impressed with the company and staff. I'm sure I could learn a lot from being a part of your team and would enjoy working with you.

The visit has convinced me that my qualifications and experience are a good match for your company. As well, I bring excellent work habits and communication skills to this position. Given the industry, I'm sure that can only be a good thing.

I look forward to hearing from you. Thank you for your consideration.

Best wishes,

Your name

SAMPLE 2 — THANK YOU AFTER AN
INTERVIEW INFORMAL EMAIL FORMAT

Name
Title
Company name
Street Address
City, State, ZIP

Dear Mr./Ms (Last name),

Thank you for today's interview for the position of (name position) at (company name).

Your thorough explanation of the company and the position reinforced my belief that I would be a wonderful fit for the team. Given the skills and qualifications that I bring to the position, I feel confident that I should be able to hit the ground running with very little training.

I'm available for further discussions if needed. Again, thank you for taking so much time to talk to me about this wonderful opportunity.

Sincerely,

Your name

SAMPLE 3 — FORGOTTEN INFORMATION - CASUAL EMAIL FORMAT

Dear Mr./Ms. (Name),

Thank you very much for the time you spent talking with me regarding the (name the position) position available at (company name). The interview was very inspiring and I am convinced that I would be a great match for the position and the company.

I realized after the interview that I had forgotten to mention a weekend seminar I took on (topic). As this is actually related to one of the possible responsibilities you mentioned during the interview, I wanted to make sure you received this additional information. Please contact me if you any questions about this training or about any of my other qualifications.

I look forward to hearing your decision about this job and I thank you again for considering me for this position.

Best wishes,

Your Name

SAMPLE 4 — WHERE THERE ARE CONCERNS THAT NEED TO BE ADDRESSED

Name

Title

Company name

Company Street Address

City, State, ZIP

Dear Mr./Ms. (Last name),

Thank you for the time you took during today's interview for the (name) position at (company name).

The interview reinforced for me that I have the skills and personality required for this position. During the interview, I know you had some reservations about (list the concern).

I wanted to reiterate that although I may not have the years of experience you were looking for, I have done (now list any previous experience you have that could support your experience, what training you might have taken that could be added here. If you have a letter from a supervisor stating your dedication or skills, mention it now or list any volunteer activities where you might have gained some experience).

From all this experience, I am confident that I would prove to be an immediate asset to the company. Please feel free to contact me if you have any questions.

Thank you again for this wonderful opportunity and I look forward to hearing your decision regarding this position.

Warmest regards,

Your name

11. ACCEPTANCE LETTER

This type of letter is written specifically to accept a job offer.

Not everyone will need to write this type of letter. Some employers will send you a letter of offer and / or an employment contract. The letter will cover all the details of the job and you will only need to sign and return it.

Before you sign, read it carefully to make sure you understand and agree to the terms. If you don't understand or if there is something different than your understanding of the job, call the person who sent the letter and ask.

If you don't receive the type of letter requiring just your signature, which could mean you received the offer over the phone, or by email, and possibly via a standard letter format, then you will need to write a letter of acceptance.

An acceptance letter needs to clearly state that you understand your responsibilities and the remunerations of your new job.

You should have been given something, either verbal or written that gives the details of your new position. Sometimes your acceptance letter is in lieu of an employment contract, so it is necessary to lay out all the details so both parties understand what's expected.

If the offer has been made verbally it's even more important to write down everything you believe to have been stated. No two people walk away from the same conversation with the exact same impression of what had been said and understood. That's why asking for the offer in writing is a good idea. Then you have something concrete to work from.

Not all companies are big enough to have a Human Resources Department and so they may not issue a written offer. If they don't, ask for a letter or an email stating the terms. They may or may not give you one. If they don't, write down in your acceptance letter, the details that you can remember as clearly as you can. This gives you a place to start.

If what you write down is different from what the interviewer thought was the agreement, they will contact you. In this way, minor problems can be sorted out before they grow into something much larger. This is a good thing as you don't want any misinterpretations to stop you from enjoying your new position or your new relationship with the person doing the hiring.

Do keep a copy of your letter of acceptance. It's proof of the point where you started with this company. If you will be working for a large company, then it's something to help you when you come to performance evaluations and promotion discussions. This may not seem valuable at this time, but it's a marker of the job responsibilities that you started with and how they've changed over time.

When your performance evaluation rolls around, consider if certain promises were made to you in the original interview, restated in the letter, and yet never came to pass, or if the job duties and goals derailed. This letter may serve as a reminder of the job you accepted and how it's not the job you ended up doing.

These types of letters are not contracts. The letter should go into your employee file. This way, if there is a disagreement, the letter is physical proof to reinforce your argument. This is another reason to keep a copy of your letter, just in case the one you sent to the company doesn't end up in your file.

Do send the letter soon after the offer has been made as you don't want anyone to think that you are not interested, to the point that they move on to the next candidate.

WHAT GOES IN YOUR ACCEPTANCE LETTER?

When writing this letter, be sure to address the letter to the person who offered you the job. If you've received the offer in writing, then you will have the information to copy. However, if you've received the offer over the phone and are uncertain of how to correctly spell the person's name, then call the company and ask.

In your acceptance letter, be sure to include:

1. Your contact information.

2. Thanks and appreciation for the opportunity.

3. Written acceptance of the offer.

4. Your new job title.

5. The start date.

6. The location where you will be working.

7. Your salary and potential bonuses.

8. Your job responsibilities.

9. A relocation package.

10. Future opportunities for growth.

Be sure to make your letter enthusiastic and friendly. Don't gush, instead be real. This letter should be a pleasant brief summary. Even though you've already been offered the job, you want to make this letter professional.

Be sure to sign the letter.

Then make a copy for your own records and send it back to the company. In today's world of electronics, if they sent you the offer by email, then you can send your letter of acceptance back the same way, providing they didn't request a hard copy signed and mailed back. If the offer was sent to you in the mail, then send the acceptance letter back the same way.

Regardless of the method you choose, wait several days, then call and confirm that they have received it. You could also send the letter via certified mail or through another tracking method so that you have confirmation that the letter has been received.

SAMPLE 1 — ACCEPTANCE LETTER TO MAIL

Your name
Street address
City, State, ZIP
Your email

Date

Full name
Title
Company
Street address
City, State, ZIP

Dear Mr./Ms. (Last name),
Thank you for the offer confirming our telephone conversation on (date). I am delighted to accept the position of (name position title) working with (give supervisor name if you know it) from the (give department name).

As discussed, the conditions of my employment include an annual salary of (list the salary) and (now list any employment benefits in the offer) specified in your offer dated (give the full date on the letter).

I'm looking forward to joining (company name) on (put in official start date) at (put in start time).

Again, thank you for the offer.

Sincerely,

Signature
Your name

SAMPLE 2 — ACCEPTANCE LETTER FORMAL EMAIL

Name
Title
Company
City, State, ZIP
Phone number with area code

Dear Mr./Ms. (Last name),

As per our phone conversation, I am pleased to accept the position of (name title) at (company name). I appreciate the opportunity and I look forward to my new future as part of your team.

As agreed on, my starting salary will be $_____. My full health and dental insurance benefits will be provided after I have completed 3 months employment.

I appreciate being chosen for this position and will show up on my start date of (put in full date). Should you need anything before this date, please feel free to contact me.

Full name

Contact information

12. REJECTION LETTERS

This type of letter is used to thank an employer for the offer of a job but ultimately rejecting it. It's a bad news letter written in a good way.

In general, the best thing to do is to phone the person who sent you the offer and explain that you are going to decline the job offer. This allows him a chance to move to the next person on the list and he will appreciate the quick response.

The phone call is then followed up with a letter. There are some schools of thought that believe only a written and mailed letter is professional for something like this. However, times are changing and many HR departments depend on email solely. Email is perfectly fine if all your correspondence with the company up to this point has been via email. It's also fine to ask how the company would like the follow up letter when you're on the phone.

You want the tone of your letter to be diplomatic, polite, and professional. Even though you are turning down a job offer from the company at this time, you don't know what the future will bring. Be sure to write the letter in such a way that you don't close this door. You may be happy to work for the company at another time.

Many people can't be bothered to write a letter to decline a job. They choose the job they want and ignore any other offers. This is not only bad form professionally, but it's also rude. You've left the other company hanging at a point in time when they need to find an alternative candidate.

Once you've made your decision to decline the offer, call if you choose to, and send the letter as soon as possible. It doesn't matter if you send the letter in the mail or by email, it still needs to be written in a professional format. It must be concise and professional.

There are two different schools of thought when it comes to giving a reason for declining the job offer in your letter. You may have given the person a reason on the phone, in which case you could restate it in the letter. Some professionals like to know so they can improve the situation next time. Your feedback helps them to understand why they aren't attracting their prime candidates. If there are many things wrong with the offer, and you don't know how to say anything positive about it, it's best to say nothing at all. Give a blanket statement and let it go at that.

However, if you can give specifics, such as another company has offered you better professional development opportunities or is closer to home so you won't have to relocate for example, then let them know. Don't tell them they wanted you to work your life away at slave labor wages. It's important to keep the overall tone of the letter positive.

WHAT GOES IN A REJECTION LETTER?

Be professional all the way. Be sure to:

1. Address the letter to the person who offered you the position.

2. Include your contact information.

3. Say thank you and show appreciation for having received the offer.

4. Give a clear rejection of the job offer.

5. Give a reason, even if only to say you've accepted another position elsewhere.

6. Offer best wishes for finding another person for the job – feel free to suggest someone if you know a person with similar qualifications.

7. Proofread the letter before sending.

SAMPLE 1 — JOB REJECTION LETTER IN STANDARD LETTER FOR MAILING

Your name
Your current address
City, State, ZIP
Email address

Name
Job title
Company
Street address
City, State, ZIP

Date

Dear Mr./Ms. (Last name),

Thank you very much for offering me the position of (put in name of position) with (put in the company's name).

After careful consideration, I have decided to decline your offer. I have accepted a different position that I feel is a better match for my career goals.

Again, thank you for your consideration.

Signature

Your name

SAMPLE 2 — SAMPLE REJECTION LETTER FOR EMAILING

Name
Organization
Street address
City, State, ZIP

Dear Mr./Ms. (Last name),

Thank you very much for your job offer to work as the General Office Manager at your company. Unfortunately, I am declining your offer as it doesn't follow the career path that I am hoping to achieve.

Thank you for taking the time to consider my application and I'm sorry it didn't work out. I wish you the best in finding someone suitable for the position.

Your name

SAMPLE 3 — REJECTION LETTER WITH A
REASON IN FORMAL EMAIL FORMAT

Name
Title
Organization
Street address
City, State, ZIP
Email address

Dear Mr./Ms. (Last name),

Thank you for offering me the position of (Position title) at (Company name). After careful deliberation, I regretfully decline your offer because (put down your reason).

I thank you for considering me and I wish you the best in finding the right person for the job.

Sincerely,

Your name
Contact information

13. COVER LETTER CHECKLIST

I t is very important to go over your letter several times to make sure you have written the most powerful cover letter possible.

Here is a basic checklist to help you:

1. Is the letter in standard business format?

2. Is it on standard paper?

3. Have you individualized the letter to a position or a person?

4. Is it easy to see where you can be reached during business hours? Do you have voicemail or an answering machine in the event you are not available?

5. Is the letter easy to read?

6. Is it one page?

7. Does the page look neat and tidy and easy to read?

8. Is it free of spelling and grammar errors?

9. Did you explain why you are contacting the person?

10. Will your first paragraph grab the reader's attention?

11. Have you used action words to convey your abilities?

12. Did you sign it? Is your signature confident and clear?

13. Have you double checked your word choices? Did you use action verbs?

14. Have you removed any repetition, and left only what is relevant?

15. Have you avoided using clichés and weak phrases like 'I believe'?

16. Is the letter appealing to read?

17. Is the tone friendly and does it show some personality?

18. Read the letter as if you were the intended audience – does it tell you what you need to know? Would you want to speak with this person further?

19. Does it answer the requirements of the position?

20. Does the letter show confidence, not arrogance?

21. Have you listed examples of your accomplishments?

22. Have you avoided listing job duties?

23. Have you shown knowledge of the company you are writing to?

24. Have you discussed your concept fully or skimped on necessary details?

25. Have you avoided discussing anything in a negative manner?

26. Have you focused the letter on what you can do for the company instead of what the company can do for you?

27. Have you avoided sounding desperate? You don't want to say 'willing to do anything required' for instance.

28. Have you done your best to highlight your university experience and unpaid work if you don't have years of experience to draw upon?

29. Have you added information instead of just rewriting what is on your resume?

30. Have you closed with a call to action stating that you will follow up by calling within a specific time frame?

CONCLUSION

Writing a cover letter is another step in your journey to a new career. The process isn't difficult but the analyzing of one's skills and accomplishments can be.

Identifying your strengths, writing them in a powerful way in order to communicate them to an employer is important, as is having a dynamite opening and an action closing to your letter, and the body is full of useful relevant information that answers the employer's needs.

Now that you have made it this far you are almost ready to send off your application. Before you do, take one more look at it, run through the checklist, and make sure it's as perfect as can be. Make it the strongest marketing tool you can that is both professional and hard-hitting to get you to the next stage – the interview.

Then take a look at your resume. Is it as strong as your cover letter? Do they, together, send the same message, the right message that you want the employer to see and hear? If not, revise one or the other or both so that you are presenting yourself in the strongest possible way. Be sure to put the same time and effort into writing your resume. If you need help be sure to see my book, Career Essentials: The Resume, available now through Amazon.com.

In summary, I'd like to add that like all areas of society, change is happening in the job-hunting industry every day. Certain professions are dying even as new ones are being created. Technology has opened new doors - at the cost of shutting down many others. That's evolution on the job front.

However, the world is open and available like never before. Spread your wings and fly to a new job, a new industry, and even a new country to begin the next stage of your journey.

There is nothing stopping you but...you.

Thanks for reading this book. I hope it helped you on your journey to creating a wonderful cover letter. Good luck on your job search!

ABOUT THE AUTHOR

Dale Mayer is a researcher, technical writer, ghostwriter, and author living in the beautiful Okanagan valley in British Columbia, Canada. She has several business books published on Mortgages, Resume Writing, and Companion Gardening. As a complement to those books, she has created The Essential Series encompassing topics in Careers, and eventually Gardening, Finance, and Lifestyle.

In fiction, she writes taut psychological suspense with romance and paranormal elements. She has recently branched out into both mystery and urban fantasy books for young adult with the occasional vampire book thrown in just for fun.

Her award winning romantic suspense series (with paranormal elements) *Tuesday's Child* is out along with book 2, *Hide'n Go Seek*, and book 3, *Maddy's Floor*.

Connect with Dale Mayer Online:

Dale's Website – www.dalemayer.com

Twitter - http://twitter.com/#!/DaleMayer

Facebook - http://www.facebook.com/DaleMayer.author

If you enjoyed this book, the second and third books in the series are also available as well as a compilation of the three books together.

CAREER ESSENTIALS: THE SERIES

Career Essentials: The Résumé

In our current economic conditions, job hunters are struggling to attain the 'perfect' job. The Internet has made job hunting easier, but has made getting the job actually harder. It's so easy to apply for jobs today that employers are overwhelmed, often receiving thousands of applications per job opening.
Somehow, you have to make sure your application rises to the top of this pile. How? Through your résumé - it's the single most powerful marketing tool you have to showcase your skills and accomplishments.
Isn't it time you seek out the next step in your life?

Career Essentials: The Interview

Today's economy is tighter and more complex than ever before. With no time or money for mistakes, companies need to find the 'right' person for every position quickly and efficiently.
To have reached the interview stage is a feat in itself. Now it's critical that you not only get through the interview but that you dominate the competition. If this is the job you want, there is no room for errors, not when there are hundreds of solid candidates lined up behind you.
This is the 3rd book in the Career Essential series, and it covers all the 'essential' information you need to know about interviewing successfully and so much more. Like all the books in this series, the information presented here is concise and clearly laid out in an easily accessible style so it's fast to read and easy to follow.
Good luck!

REFERENCES

1. *A free sample declination letter*, Quintcareers.com. Accessed April 24, 2011 http://www.quintcareers.com/sample _declining_letter.html

2. Beatty, Richard H, *175 High-Impact Cover letters* (3rd ed.), 2002, John Wiley & Sons, Inc. New York, NY.

3. Campbell, Susan, *Salary History and Salary Requirements*, 1st-Writer.com. Accessed May 1, 2001 from http://www.1st-writer.com/Salary.htm

4. Campbell, Susan, *Salary negotiation skills and strategies – for navigating the rough terrain*, 1st-Writer.com. Accessed on May 1, 2011 from www.1stwriter.com/negotiation_skills.htm

5. Colorado State University. *Writing Guide: Acceptance Letters.* Accessed June 21, 2010, http://writing.colostate.edu /guides/documents/business_writing/business_letter/acc eptance_letter/.

6. Donlin, Kevin, *Resume and Cover Letter Secrets Revealed*, July 2000, Guaranteed Resumes.com, Ebook.

7. Doyle, Allison, *Cover letter referral example*, About.com. Accessed on March 28, 2011 from http://jobsearch.about .com/od/samplenetworkingletters/a/cover-letter-referred.htm

8. Doyle, Allison, *Email cover letter format*, About.com. Accessed on April 10, 2011 from http://jobsearch.about. com/od/emailcoverlettersamples/qt/email-cover-letter-format.htm

9. Doyle Allison, *Sample email networking message*, About.com. Accessed on April 24, 2011 from http://jobsearch.about. om/od/samplenetworkingletters/a/networkingmessage.h tm

10. Doyle, Allison, *Sample job rejection letter*, About.com. Accessed April 2, 2011 from http://jobsearch.about.com /od/morejobletters/a/jobreject2.htm

11. Doyle, Allison, *Sample student career networking letter*, About.com. Accessed on April 13, 2011 from http://jobsearch.about.com/cs/networking/a/networkin g_3.htm

12. Doyle, Allison, *Types of cover letters*, About.com. Accessed on March 22, 2011 from http://jobsearch.about.com /od/coverletters/a/types-of-cover-letters.htm.

13. Enelow, Wendy S., Kursmark, Louise M., *Cover Letter Magic*, (2nd ed.) 2004, JIST Works, Indianapolis, IN

14. Frank, William S. *All endings and avoiding Sincerely*, Cover-Letters.com. Accessed April 5, 2011 from http://www.cover-letters.com/Cover-Letters/About-Cover-Letters/How-To-Write-A-Great-Letter/About-Endings-And-Avoiding-Sincerely.aspx

15. Frank, William S, *FAQ about cover letters*, Cover-letters.com. Accessed April 30, 2011 from http://www.cover-letters.com/Cover-Letters/About-Cover-Letters/How-To-Write-A-Great-Letter/FAQ-About-Cover-Letters.aspx

16. *Guide to cover letter writing*, Becker Career Center, Union College. Accessed on April 27, 2011. http://www.union.edu/StudentLife/BeckerCareerCenter

17. Job Bank USA. *How to Write an Acceptance Letter.* Accessed June 21, 2010 http://www.jobbankusa.com/interviews /articles_tips/how_to_write_an_acceptance_letter.html.

18. Kennedy, Joyce Lain, *How to begin a cover letter*, Dummies.com. Accessed April 12, 2011 from http://www.dummies.com/how-to/content/how-to-begin-a-cover-letter.seriesId-135244.html

19. Kennedy, Joyce Lain, *How to close a cover letter*, Dummies.com. Accessed April 14, 2011 from http://www.dummies.com/how-to/content/how-to-close-a-cover-letter.seriesId-135244.html

20. Kennedy, Joyce Lain, *Punctuation fundamentals for cover letters.* Accessed April 13, 2011, from http://www.dummies.com

/how-to/content/punctuation-fundamentals-for-cover-letters.seriesId-135244.html

21. Kennedy, Joyce Lain, *Tips for writing strong cover letters,* Dummies.com. Accessed April 13, 2011 from http://www.dummies.com/how-to/content/tips-for-writing-strong-cover-letters.seriesId-135244.html

22. Newberger, Nathan, *Tips for writing cover letters,* WorkTree.com. Accessed April 22, 2011, from http://www.worktree.com/tb/CL_tips.cfm

23. Paxton, Sandra, Podesta, Sandra, *201 Killer Cover Letters,* 2003, The McGraw-Hill Companies, Inc. USA.

24. Prasad, Chandra. "*Outwitting the Job Market: Everything You Need to Locate and Land a Great Position.*" Guilford, CT: Lyons Press, 2004.

25. Purdue Online Writing Lab. *Acceptance Letter.* Accessed June 21, 2010 http://owl.english.purdue.edu/owl/resource/634/06/.

26. *Sample declination letter,* CVTips, Accessed March 20, 2011 from http://www.cvtips.com/cover-letter/sample-declination-letter.html

27. Schneider, Laura, *Interview thank you letter,* About.com, Tech Careers. Accessed on April 13, 2011 from http://jobsearchtech.about.com/od/resumesandletters/a/thankyoultrs.htm

28. Stout, Kay, *Referral cover letter example.* About.com. Accessed April 19, 2011 from http://jobsearch.about.com/od/coverlettersamples/a/referralexample.htm

18676185R00068

Made in the USA
Lexington, KY
18 November 2012